Quilt Notes

Irish Chain quilts have such an orderly look with their colorful blocks marching in precision, rows angling across the quilt from top to bottom. You might think that they are easy to recognize until you do a little research. In Barbara Brackman's *Encyclopedia of Pieced Quilt Patterns* there are seven Irish Chain blocks, seven Double Irish Chain blocks and two Triple Irish Chain blocks. The variety of blocks shown is amazing: some of the "chains" go up and down instead of at an angle. Some blocks are appliquéd instead of pieced.

We have narrowed the scope of this book to quilts with "chains" that angle across the quilt, crossing each other to create points of interest. Even within that category, there are plenty of variations. One quilt alternates framed Nine-Patch blocks with framed plain blocks; the point of interest is the embroidery work on the plain blocks. Another quilt alternates framed Four-Patch blocks with Framed Log Cabin blocks on point. Not all Irish Chains are created with blocks. A third quilt starts with appliquéd motifs, on a background block which is set on point. The chain is created by combining Four-Patch blocks and triangles. The fourth quilt looks like it is made out of blocks, but is actually put together in sections and rows, much as you would put together puzzle pieces. As in all the quilts, the color placement creates the chains that crisscross the quilt.

The four methods used in this book all create beautiful Irish Chain quilts. They're all fun and easy to do, so you may want to try each one. After you've decided on your favorite method, you'll be ready to make Irish Chain quilts for family and friends. By changing the motifs, blocks and colors, you can easily create your own original Irish Chain quilts!

E-mail: Customer_Service@whitebirches.com

HOUSE of WHITE BIRCHES
PUBLISHERS SINCE 1947

Irish Chain Made Easy is published by House of White Birches, 306 East Parr Road, Berne, IN 46711, telephone (260) 589-4000. Printed in USA. Copyright © 2005 House of White Birches.

RETAILERS: If you would like to carry this pattern book or any other House of White Birches publications, call the Wholesale Department at Annie's Attic to set up a direct account: (903) 636-4303. Also, request a complete listing of publications available from House of White Birches.

Every effort has been made to ensure that the instructions in this pattern book are complete and accurate. We cannot, however, take responsibility for human error, typographical mistakes or variations in individual work.

STAFF
Editors: Jeanne Stauffer, Sandra L. Hatch
Associate Editor: Dianne Schmidt
Technical Artist: Connie Rand
Copy Supervisor: Michelle Beck
Copy Editors: Nicki Lehman, Mary Martin, Beverly Richardson
Graphic Arts Supervisor: Ronda Bechinski

Graphic Artists: Debby Keel, Edith Teegarden
Art Director: Brad Snow
Assistant Art Director: Nick Pierce
Photography: Tammy Christian, Carl Clark, Christena Green, Matt Owen
Photo Stylist: Tammy Nussbaum

ISBN: 1-59217-046-3
1 2 3 4 5 6 7 8 9

Lucky Shamrocks

BY DIANA DIPAOLO

The luck of the Irish will be with you as you quilt this Irish treasure.

Project Specifications

Skill Level: Beginner
Wall Quilt Size: 31½" x 31½"
Block Size: 7½" x 7½"
Number of Blocks: 9

Fabric & Batting

- ¾ yard each light and dark prints
- 1 yard medium print
- Backing 37" x 37"
- Batting 37" x 37"
- 3¾ yards self-made or purchased binding

Supplies & Tools

- Neutral color all-purpose thread
- 1 spool green quilting thread
- Basic sewing supplies and tools

Instructions

1. Cut the following strips in sizes given: light print—one strip 2" by fabric width, two strips 5" x 22" and four strips 2" x 22"; medium print—four strips 2" x 22" and five strips 2" by fabric width; and dark print—four strips 2" by fabric width and one strip 2" x 22".

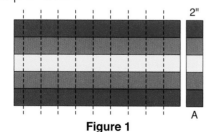

Figure 1
Cut (10) 2" segments for A as shown.

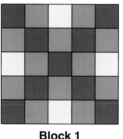

Block 1
7½" x 7½"

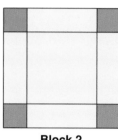

Block 2
7½" x 7½"

2. Join one light, two medium and two dark 2" by fabric width strips together along length to make A segments. Cut stitched section in 2" segments referring to Figure 1; you will need 10 A segments.

3. Sew three medium and two dark 2" by fabric width strips together along length to make B segments. Cut stitched section in 2" segments referring to Figure 2; you will need 10 B segments.

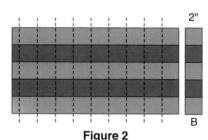

Figure 2
Cut (10) 2" segments for B as shown.

4. Sew one dark, two medium and two light 2" x 22" fabric strips together along length to make C segments. Cut stitched section in 2"

segments referring to Figure 3; you will need five C segments.

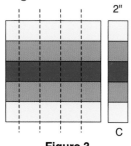
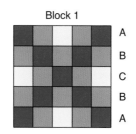

Figure 3
Cut five 2" segments for C as shown.

Figure 4
Join A, B and C segments to make Block 1.

5. Arrange two A, two B and one C segment together in rows referring to Figure 4; join rows to complete Block 1; repeat for five blocks. Press and square up to 8" x 8".

6. Sew one light 5" x 22" strip between two medium 2" x 22" strips along length to make D segments. Cut stitched section in 2" segments referring to Figure 5; you will need eight D segments.

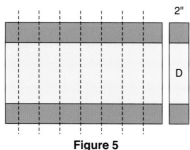

Figure 5
Cut eight 2" segments for D as shown.

7. Sew one light 5" x 22" strip between two light 2" x 22" strips along length to make E segments. Cut stitched section in 5" segments referring to Figure 6; you will need four E segments.

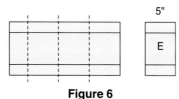

Figure 6
Cut four 5" segments for E as shown.

8. Sew two D segments to each E segment to make Block 2 as shown in Figure 7; repeat for four blocks. Press and square up to 8" x 8".

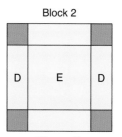

Figure 7
Join E and D segments to make Block 2 as shown.

9. Arrange Blocks 1 and 2 in rows referring to Figure 8. Join in rows; join rows to complete pieced center; press.

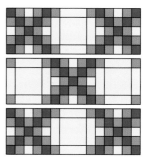

Figure 8
Arrange blocks in rows as shown.

10. Cut two strips dark print 2" x 23"; sew a strip to opposite sides of pieced center. Press seams toward strips. Cut two strips dark print 2" x 26"; sew a strip to remaining opposite sides. Press seams toward strips.

11. Using leftover 2" x 2" pieces, create four Four-Patch squares for corners referring to Figure 9.

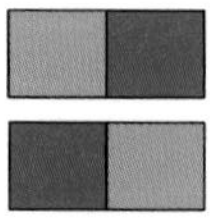

Figure 9
Make Four-Patch corner blocks as shown.

12. Cut four strips medium print 3½" x 26"; sew a strip to opposite sides of pieced center. Press seams toward strips. Sew a Four-Patch square to each end of the remaining two strips. Sew a strip to remaining opposite sides; press seams toward strips.

13. Mark quilting design given in the center of the light print squares referring to Placement Diagram and project for positioning.

Finishing the Quilt

1. Sandwich batting between the completed top and the prepared backing piece; pin or baste to hold. Quilt the marked design and other areas of the quilt as desired.

2. Trim backing and batting even with top. Remove pins or basting.

3. Bind with self-made or purchased binding to finish. ∎

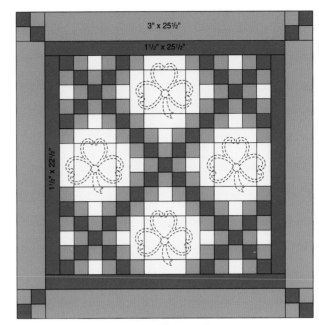

Lucky Shamrock
Placement Diagram
31½" x 31½"

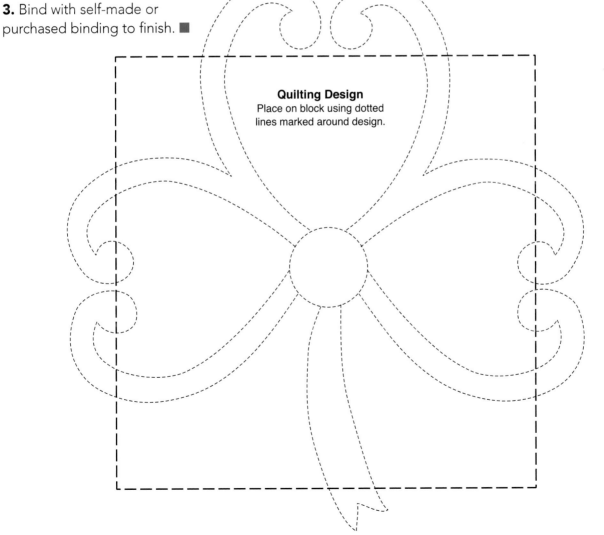

Quilting Design
Place on block using dotted
lines marked around design.

Irish Chain Cabins

BY RUTH SWASEY

Log Cabin blocks set with Framed Four-Patch blocks create the appearance of an Irish Chain quilt.

Project Specifications
Skill Level: Beginner
Quilt Size: 84" x 96"
Block Size: 12" x 12"
Number of Blocks: 35

Fabric & Batting
- Scrap strips red and blue prints to total 1½ yards each
- ⅔ yard red print for binding
- ⅞ yard red-and-white print
- ⅞ yard blue tone-on-tone
- 1 yard patriotic print
- 1 yard flag print
- 3½ yards white-on-white print
- Backing 90" x 102"
- Batting 90" x 102"

Supplies & Tools
- Neutral color all-purpose thread
- Quilting thread
- Basic sewing tools and supplies

Piecing Log Cabin Blocks
1. Cut 17 squares patriotic print 2" x 2" for block centers.

2. Trim red and blue print scrap strips to varying widths from 1¼" to 2".

3. Sew red print strips to opposite sides of a center square; press and trim referring to Figure 1. Repeat on remaining sides with blue

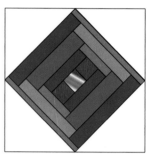

Framed Four-Patch
12" x 12" Block

Framed Log Cabin
12" x 12" Block

print strips in the same manner. Continue to add red strips to opposite sides and blue strips to the remaining sides to create 17 Courthouse Steps–style Log Cabin units as shown in Figure 2. **Note:** *The size does not matter at this time.*

Figure 1
Sew red print strips to opposite sides of a center square.

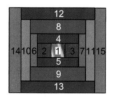

Figure 2
Sew strips to the center square to complete 1 Log Cabin unit.

Figure 3
Trim all Log Cabin units to 9" x 9".

4. Trim all Log Cabin units to 9" x 9" as shown in Figure 3. **Note:** *The outside strips on each block will be of varying widths.*

5. Cut eight strips 6⅞" by fabric width white-on-white print; subcut into (48) 6⅞" square segments. Cut each square on one diagonal to make A triangles; set aside 28 A triangles for side triangle units.

6. Sew an A triangle to each side of the trimmed Log Cabin units to complete one Framed Log Cabin block as shown in Figure 4. Repeat for 17 blocks; press seams toward A.

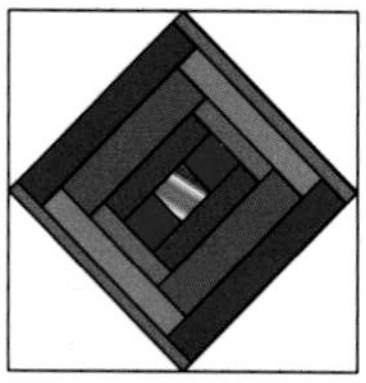

Figure 4
Sew an A triangle to each side of the trimmed Log Cabin unit to complete 1 Framed Log Cabin block.

Piecing Framed Four-Patch Blocks

1. Cut eight strips each red-and-white print (D) and blue tone-on-tone (E) 3½" by fabric width. Join one strip of each color with right sides together along length; repeat for four strip sets. Press seams toward darker fabric. Set aside remaining strips for step 4 and for completing border patch units.

2. Subcut strip sets into 3½" segments for B as shown in Figure 5; you will need 54 B segments. Set aside 10 for side units.

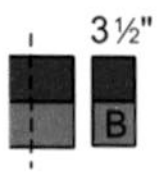

Figure 5
Subcut strip sets into 3½" segments for B.

Figure 6
Join 2 B segments to make a B unit.

3. Join two B segments to make a B unit as shown in Figure 6; repeat for 22 units. Set aside four B units for border corners.

4. Cut seven strips white-on-white print 6½" by fabric width for C. Center a C strip between one D and one E strip set aside in step 1; press seams away from C. Repeat for four D-C-E strip sets.

5. Subcut the D-C-E strip sets into 3½" segments as shown in Figure 7; you will need 46 segments. Set aside 10 segments for border patch units.

6. Subcut (36) 3½" C segments from the remaining C strips.

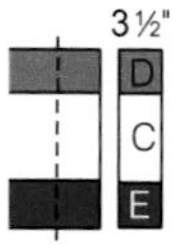

Figure 7
Subcut the D-C-E strip sets into 3½" segments.

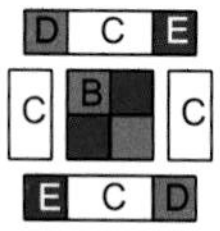

Figure 8
Join units to complete 1 block.

7. To complete one Framed Four-Patch block, sew C to opposite sides of a B unit referring to Figure 8; press seams toward C. Add a D-C-E unit to the long sides of the B-C unit to complete the block, again referring to Figure 8; press seams away from center unit. Repeat for 18 blocks.

Completing the Top

1. Cut four 13¼" x 13¼" squares patriotic print for F. Cut each F square in half on both diagonals to make F triangles. Discard two F triangles.

2. Sew an A triangle to two adjacent sides of F to make an A-F side triangle unit as shown in Figure 9; repeat for 14 A-F units. Press seams toward A.

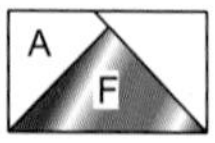

Figure 9
Sew an A triangle to 2 adjacent sides of F to complete an A-F unit.

3. Cut two strips white-on-white print 3½" by fabric width for G; subcut strips into (20) 3½" G squares.

4. Sew a G square to each end of a B segment as shown in Figure 10; press seams toward B. Sew a D-C-E unit to the G-B-G unit to complete one border patch unit, again referring to Figure 10. Repeat for 10 units, again referring to Figure 10 for positioning of the red and blue pieces.

Figure 10
Complete border patch
units as shown.

5. Arrange and join three Framed Four-Patch blocks with two Framed Log Cabin blocks and two A-F units to make an X row referring to Figure 11; repeat for four X rows. Press seams toward Framed Four-Patch blocks.

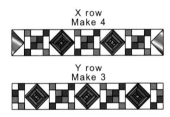

Figure 11
Join blocks to make X and Y rows.

6. Arrange and join three Framed Log Cabin blocks with two Framed Four-Patch blocks and two border patch units to make a Y row, again referring to Figure 11; repeat for three Y rows. Press seams toward Framed Four-Patch blocks.

7. Join the rows referring to the Placement Diagram; press seams in one direction.

8. Join two B units with three A-F units and two border patch units to make a Z row as shown in

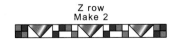

Figure 12
Join units to make a Z row.

Figure 12; repeat for two Z rows. Press seams toward B and border patch units.

9. Sew a Z row to the top and bottom of the pieced center referring to the Placement Diagram for positioning of rows; press seams toward Z rows.

10. Cut and piece two 6½" x 96½" H strips white flag print. Sew an H strip to opposite long sides of the pieced center; press seams toward H.

Finishing the Quilt
1. Prepare quilt top for quilting and quilt.

2. When quilting is complete, trim batting and backing edges even with the quilted top.

3. Prepare 10½ yards red print binding and bind edges of quilt to finish. ▪

Irish Chain Cabins
Placement Diagram
84" x 96"

Deer Crossing

BY JUDITH SANDSTROM

The sportsman in your life would love this masculine-looking wall quilt.

Project Specifications
Skill Level: Beginner
Quilt Size: 48" x 48"
Block Size: 11¼" x 11¼"
Number of Blocks: 4

Fabric & Batting
- ½ yard medium blue mottled
- ⅜ yard black mottled
- ⅝ yard navy/tan plaid
- 1 yard navy mottled
- 1¼ yards tan-on-tan print
- Batting 54" x 54"
- Backing 54" x 54"

Supplies & Tools
- Neutral color and black all-purpose thread
- Tan quilting thread
- ½ yard fusible web
- ⅔ yard fabric stabilizer
- Basic sewing tools and supplies

Making Appliqué Blocks
1. Cut four 11¾" x 11¾" A squares tan-on-tan print; fold and crease to mark diagonal centers.

2. Trace the deer pattern on the paper side of the fusible web four times. **Note:** *The pattern is already reversed.*

3. Cut out shapes, leaving a margin around each one; fuse shapes to the wrong side of the black mottled. Cut out shapes on traced lines; remove paper backing.

4. Center a deer shape diagonally on A; fuse in place. Repeat for four blocks.

Deer
11¼" x 11¼" Block

5. Cut an 11" x 11" square fabric stabilizer; pin a square behind each fused A square.

6. Using black all-purpose thread, machine zigzag-stitch around each deer shape. When stitching is complete, remove fabric stabilizer.

Completing the Top
1. Cut five 2½" by fabric width strips each navy and medium blue mottleds.

2. Sew a navy mottled strip to a medium blue mottled strip with right sides together along length; press seams open. Repeat for five strip sets.

3. Subcut strip sets into 2½" B segments as shown in Figure 1; you will need 80 B segments.

Figure 1
Subcut strip sets into 2½" B segments.

4. Join two B segments as shown in Figure 2 to make B units; press seams open. Repeat for 40 B units. Set aside four B units for borders.

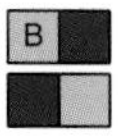

Figure 2
Join 2 B segments to make B units.

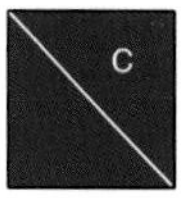

Figure 3
Cut each C square in half on 1 diagonal to make C triangles.

5. Cut three 4⅞" by fabric width strips navy mottled; subcut strips into 4⅞" C squares. You will need 24 squares. Cut each C square in half on one diagonal to make 48 C triangles as shown in Figure 3.

6. Sew a C triangle to a B unit as shown in Figure 4; press seams open. Repeat for 36 B-C units.

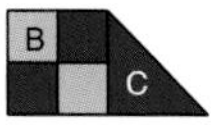

Figure 4
Sew a C triangle to a B unit.

Figure 5
Stitch a second C triangle to B-C units.

7. Stitch a second C triangle to four B-C units as shown in Figure 5; press seams open. Set aside for P units.

8. Join two B-C units as shown in Figure 6 to make M units; repeat for 12 M units. Press seams open.

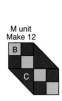

Figure 6
Join 2 B-C units to make an M unit.

Figure 7
Sew C to an M unit to make an N unit.

9. Sew C to four M units to make N units as shown in Figure 7; press seams open.

10. Sew C to four M units to make O units as shown in Figure 8.

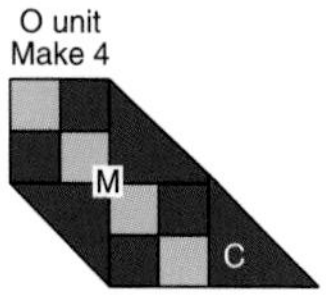

Figure 8
Sew C to an M unit to make an O unit.

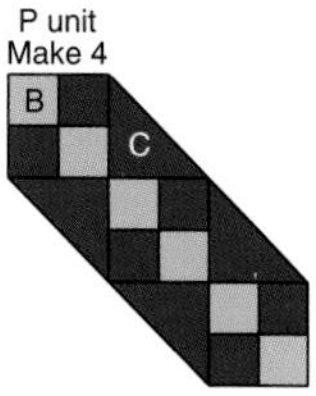

Figure 9
Join 2 B-C units with a C-B-C unit to make a P unit.

11. Join two B-C units with a C-B-C unit set aside in step 7 to make a P unit as shown in Figure 9; press seams open; repeat for four P units.

12. Cut two 9¼" x 9¼" D squares tan-on-tan print. Cut each D square in half on both diagonals to make D triangles as shown in Figure 10.

Figure 10
Cut D in half on both diagonals to make D triangles.

13. Sew a D triangle to opposite sides of each remaining M unit as shown in Figure 11.

14. Lay out the pieced units with the appliquéd blocks referring to Figure 12; join units using set-in seams where necessary; press seams open.

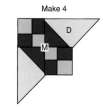

Figure 11
Sew a D triangle to opposite sides of an M unit.

15. Cut four 4½" x 40½" E strips navy/tan plaid.

16. Sew an E strip to opposite sides of the pieced center; press

Figure 12
Lay out the pieced units with the appliquéd blocks; join using set-in seams where necessary.

seams toward strips. Sew the remaining B units to each end of each remaining E strip; press seams open.

17. Sew the B-E strips to the remaining sides of the pieced center; press seams open.

Finishing the Quilt

1. Sandwich batting between the completed top and prepared backing piece; pin or baste layers together to hold flat for quilting.

2. Quilt as desired by hand or machine. ***Note:*** *The quilt shown was hand-quilted ¼" from seams using tan quilting thread.*

3. When quilting is complete, trim batting and backing even with quilted top; remove pins or basting.

4. Cut five 2¼" by fabric width strips tan-on-tan print; join strips on short ends to make one long strip for binding.

5. Fold the binding strip in half along length with wrong sides together; press.

6. Sew binding strip to quilt edge with raw edges matching, mitering corners and overlapping beginning and end; turn to backside. Hand-or machine-stitch in place to finish. ■

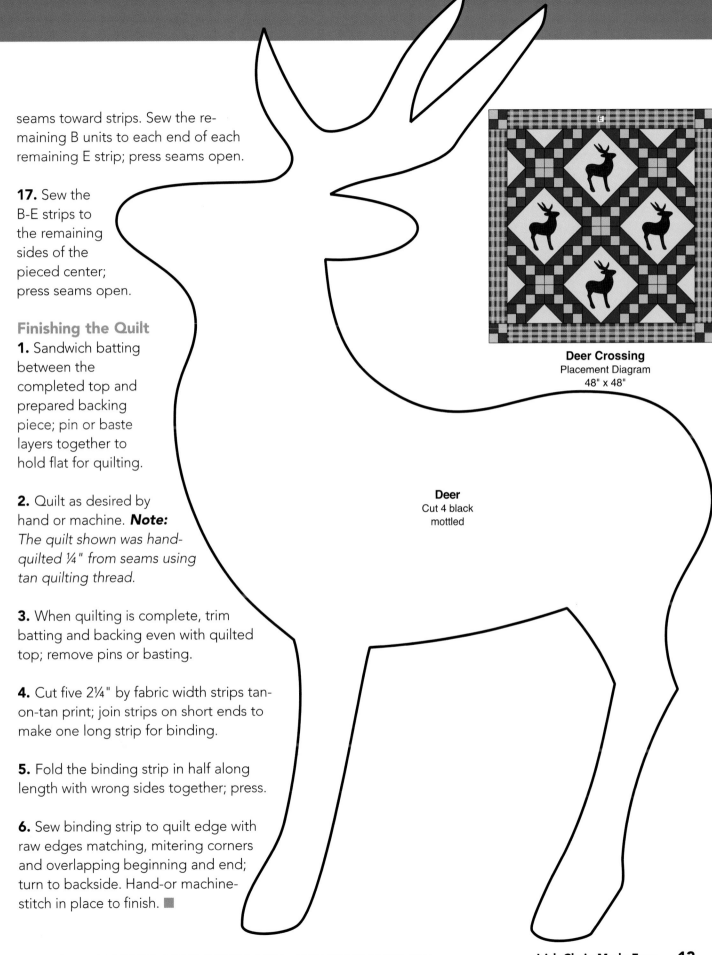

Deer Crossing
Placement Diagram
48" x 48"

Deer
Cut 4 black
mottled

Garden Pathways

BY JUDITH SANDSTROM

This quilt is not made in blocks but in sections, so constructing the top is like putting puzzle pieces together.

Project Specifications
Skill Level: Beginner
Quilt Size: 82¾" x 102¼"

Fabrics & Batting
- ½ yard each purple and lavender prints
- 1⅛ yards dark green print
- 1¼ yards light green print
- 1¼ yards green-and-purple print
- 4½ yards cream-on-cream print
- Batting 88" x 108"
- Backing 88" x 108"
- 10¾ yards self-made or purchased binding

Supplies & Tools
- All-purpose thread to match fabrics
- Cream quilting thread
- Basic sewing supplies and tools, rotary cutter, mat and ruler

Instructions

1. Cut 33 strips cream-on-cream print 3¾" by fabric width; set aside 13 strips. Subcut eight strips into 3¾" square segments for A; you will need 84 A squares. Subcut 12 strips into 10¼" segments for B; you will need 45 B pieces.

2. Cut eight strips each light green and cream-on-cream prints 4⅛" by fabric width; subcut each strip into 4⅛" square segments. You will need 80 squares of each fabric. Cut each square in half on one diagonal to make C triangles; you will need 160 C triangles of each fabric.

3. Sew a cream-on-cream print C to a light green print C as shown in Figure 1; repeat for all C triangles to make 160 C units. Set aside.

Figure 1
Sew a cream-on-cream prin C to a light green print C.

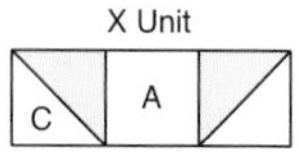

Figure 2
Join 2 C units with an A square to make an X unit.

4. Join two C units with an A square to make an X unit as shown in Figure 2; repeat for 80 X units.

5. Join B with two X units as shown in Figure 3 to make one Y unit; repeat for 31 Y units.

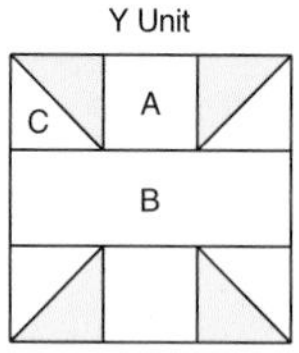

Figure 3
Join B with 2 X units to make a Y unit.

6. Cut four strips each purple and lavender prints, and nine strips dark green print 3¾" by fabric width.

7. Join strips with cream-on-cream print strips set aside in step 1 with right sides together along length in the following color combinations to make strip sets: purple/cream/purple—make 2; lavender/cream/lavender—make 2; dark green/cream/dark green—make 3; and cream/dark green/cream—make 3. Press seams toward darker fabric.

8. Subcut each strip set into 3¾" segments as shown in Figure 4.

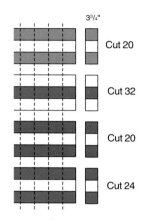

3¾"

Cut 20

Cut 32

Cut 20

Cut 24

Figure 4
Subcut each strip set
into 3¾" segments.

9. Join segments to make Nine-Patch units as shown in Figure 5.

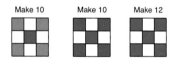

Make 10   Make 10   Make 12

Figure 5
Join segments to make
Nine-Patch units as shown.

10. Referring to Figure 6, arrange and join pieces and units in horizontal rows; press seams open.

Rows 1 and 11

Rows 2, 4, 6, 8 and 10

Rows 3, 5, 7 and 9

Figure 6
Arrange and join pieces and units in horizontal rows.

11. Arrange the pieced rows in numerical order referring to the Placement Diagram for positioning of rows; join rows to complete the pieced center. Press seams open.

12. Cut and piece two strips each green-and-purple print 4½" x 75¼" and 4½" x 94¾" and four squares dark green print 4½" x 4½". Sew the longer strips to opposite long sides of the pieced center; press seams toward strips. Sew a square to each end of the remaining two strips; sew to the top and bottom of the pieced center. Press seams toward strips.

13. Sandwich batting between the completed top and the prepared backing piece; pin or baste to hold. Quilt as desired. **Note:** *The sample shown was hand-quilted using cream quilting thread.*

14. Trim backing and batting even with top. Remove pins or basting.

15. Bind with self-made or purchased binding to finish. ■

4" x 4"

4" x 74¾"

4" x 94¼"

Garden Pathways
Placement Diagram
82¾" x 102¼"